The Mosaics of the National Shrine of the Immaculate Conception

I. CHRIST IN MAJESTY *(detail)*

The Mosaics of the National Shrine of the Immaculate Conception

By Frank DiFederico

DECATUR HOUSE PRESS
WASHINGTON, D.C.

Library of Congress Cataloging in Publication Data

DiFederico, Frank
    The mosaics of the National Shrine of the Immaculate Conception.

    Includes index.
    1. Mosaics—Washington, D.C. 2. Christian art and symbolism—Modern period,
1500-   —Washington, D.C. 3. Washington, D.C. National Shrine of the Immaculate
Conception. I. Title.
NA3840.D53 1981   738.5'2'09753   80–28403
ISBN 0–916276–09–0

                        Decatur House Press, Ltd.
                        2122 Decatur Place, NW
                        Washington, D.C. 20008

Contents

Abbreviations

CC   *Crypt Contracts. Retired File.* Archives of the National Shrine of the Immaculate Conception.

CS   *Construction Schedule.* Archives of the National Shrine of the Immaculate Conception.

EH   *Events and Happenings.* Archives of the National Shrine of the Immaculate Conception.

Kennedy William P. Kennedy. *National Shrine of the Immaculate Conception. Book I. Story of the Crypt.* Washington, D.C. [1927].

MS   *Mary's Shrine.* Quarterly bulletin published by the National Shrine of the Immaculate Conception, May 1959–.

SR   *Salve Regina.* Quarterly bulletin published by the National Shrine of the Immaculate Conception, January 1914–February 1959.

Illustrations

Preface

My work on the mosaic decorations in the National Shrine of the Immaculate Conception in Washington, D.C. began a few years ago on my return from Rome where I had just completed my research on the mosaics in St. Peter's. The decorations there span from the late sixteenth century to the present. In the course of my study I realized how little one knows of the history and the development of post-Byzantine mosaics, even though, starting with those in St. Peter's, there are a large number of examples—S. Paolo fuori le Mura in Rome, Sacré Coeur in Paris, Westminster Cathedral in London, St. Louis Cathedral, the Library of Congress in Washington, D.C.—which testify that the medium survived the Renaissance and continued to be employed with skill and vitality into the twentieth century. I decided that one way of filling this gap in our knowledge of the history of art was to focus on one of the most complete and most impressive ensembles of modern mosaics in this country, those in the National Shrine of the Immaculate Conception, and to study them within the context of the tradition to which they rightfully belong. My hope is that this modest work will inspire other scholars to look back at the mosaics executed in Europe and the Americas in the past few centuries and to find in them a fruitful and worthwhile area of investigation.

I wish to express my thanks and appreciation to the many people who have aided and encouraged my study. The book could never have been ac-

ix

tualized without the help and interest of the Reverend Monsignor John J. Murphy, Director of the National Shrine of the Immaculate Conception, and John Connelly, Director of Public Relations and Development. I am deeply grateful to both of them and their staffs, particularly William Grillo, Assistant to the Director, and Frances Green, Executive Secretary to the Director, for their enthusiasm and support.

I corresponded and met personally with a number of artists, colleagues, and friends who were either directly involved with the mosaic decorations in the National Shrine or with some other facet of my project. Among them are Costante Crovatto of Crovatto Mosaics, Yonkers, New York; John de Rosen; Albinas Elskus; Arno Heuduck of the Ravenna Mosaic Company, St. Louis, Missouri; Vytautas K. Jonynas; Aleksandra Kasuba; Eugene F. Kennedy, Jr., Architect of the National Shrine; Henry A. La-Farge; Barbara Lazo of the Old Warsaw Gallery, Alexandria, Virginia; Eda Levantine, Associate Professor and Chairman, French Department, Trinity College; Sister Columba Mullaly, retired Vice-President, Trinity College; Mary A. Reardon; Marie Spiro, Associate Professor of Art History, University of Maryland; Sister Thoma Swanson, Albertus Magnus College; and Jim Yarnall. All were unstinting with their time and knowledge, and extremely informative. Without their generosity my study would have been a great deal more difficult to complete.

Washington, D.C.   F.D.
November 1980

x

For my mother
Maria Canosa DiFederico

*The Mosaics of the National Shrine
of the Immaculate Conception*

The National Shrine of the Immaculate Conception in Washington, D.C. contains one of the most impressive displays of mosaics to be found in the United States. The mosaics cover the walls of the apses and the chapels, the vaults, and the domes of the building, and they are used as altarpieces on all the principal altars in both the upper and lower churches. With few exceptions the pictorial decorations of the Shrine are all done in mosaic, and the ensemble adds color and brilliance to the interior of the church.

A monumental church in Washington dedicated to the Mother of Jesus under the title of her Immaculate Conception was advanced by Bishop Thomas Shahan, Rector of the Catholic University of America, in 1914, supporting an idea that went back to 1846 when a council of bishops assembled in Baltimore proposed that the Blessed Virgin be made Patroness of the United States.[1] At that time, the plans were for a Gothic church which by its very nature would have excluded mosaics. But fortunately, those plans were revised and in 1919, when the Boston architectural firm of Maginnis and Walsh, in association with Frederick V. Murphy, Professor of Architecture at Catholic University, was put in charge of the project, it was decided to execute the church in a Byzantine manner.

According to some notes made at a later date by Mr. Maginnis, the Gothic was rejected because a plan with long aisles and a long nave would

I

hamper the functions of the building as a shrine church. In addition, the Gothic provided no precedent for the large crypt which was to be part of the program of the National Shrine. The fact that the Gothic style was being used for the Episcopal National Cathedral, which at that time was also being built in Washington, was another reason for rejecting it. Maginnis remembered that "the new Westminster Cathedral of London . . . couched in the Byzantine manner, suggested itself as a notable example of an architecture of complete integrity, whose religious adaptability was unquestionable and whose structural character was particularly favorable to an economical principle in its construction. The Gothic style intrinsically demands the simultaneous construction of the exterior and interior, [and] . . . would call for an enormous immediate expenditure. As is evidenced in the London example and in the great Basilicas of tradition, the interior treatment becomes a system of veneer which would permit a gradual development as funds became available."[2]

The original drawings of the interior of the Shrine show that the "veneer," in accordance with traditional Byzantine interior decorations like those in St. Mark's in Venice and Hagia Sophia in Istanbul—and those in Westminster Cathedral—were in large part to be done in mosaics. This is confirmed by an early source which states that "the architects have a very distinguished plan of mosaics [for the interior of the Shrine] based on the early Christian examples of Rome."[3] Perhaps no other decorative medium is as appropriate as mosaics for ornamenting churches. The use of them in the National Shrine of the Immaculate Conception links the church with some of the great monuments of Christendom, and establishes for it a kinship and an historical continuity which is rooted in the dawn of the Christian era.

Under the broad banner of a Byzantine style, the Crypt Church was to embody in its architecture, and specifically in its decorations, an "Early Romanesque" manner because it was "by far the oldest of purely Christian styles."[4] What was meant, to be more precise, is not Early Romanesque, but Early Christian, the style of buildings and decorations executed from roughly 300 to 600 A.D. The foundation stone for the building was laid on 23 September 1920, and though Mass was said in the Crypt Church on Easter Sunday of 1924 the Crypt with all its ornamentation was not completed until mid-1931.[5] The ceiling of the Crypt Church was covered with pictorial and decorative Guastavino tiles designed by Mary Chase Stratton and executed by Pewabic Potteries of Detriot. The main altar of the church is dedicated to Our Lady of the Catacombs and the low rounded vaults complimented by the gray-brownish tiles help to create a setting appropriate to that dedication by suggesting the atmosphere of the Roman catacombs and of early Christian places of worship.

The iconographic scheme of the crypt conveys in each of the three apses the themes of Promise, Fulfillment in Christ born of Mary, and Fulfillment in the Church through the Holy Spirit.[6] The scheme is rendered in the tiles and in the stained glass of the lunette windows, and it is alluded to as well by the mosaic panels designed by Bancel LaFarge for the fifteen altars set into the apses.

Originally the radiating altars were to be dedicated to the Virgin Mary. In the center of the north apse a copy of the seventeenth-century painting of the *Madonna of the Immaculate Conception* in the Louvre by Bartolomè Estaban Murillo, which had been in the chapel in Caldwell Hall at Catholic University since 1817, was to be placed. Another representation of the Immaculate Conception by Murillo, one in the Prado in Madrid, incidentally, at about this same time was being copied in mosaic by the Vatican Mosaic Studio as a gift for the Shrine. The other altars were to contain various images of the Madonna with reference to famous Marian shrines: Our Lady of Czestochowa, Poland; Our Lady of Einsiedeln, Switzerland; Our Lady of Pilar, Spain; Our Lady of Loreto, Italy. However, in 1923, the program was changed and the altars of the west and east apses were dedicated instead to famous early Christian virgin saints and martyrs.[7] The original plan, though, was not entirely lost, and it would reemerge in the 1950s in the decorations of some of the chapels in both the upper and lower church.

In the second program for the altars of the Crypt Church, four saints were to be placed flanking an image of the Virgin in the west and east apses. In November 1924 one could see on each of the altars "a broad and effective sketch of each female saint . . . painted on tapestry" executed, with one unrecorded exception, by Frederic de Henwood.[8] In the west apse, going from right to left, the saint to whom the first altar was to be dedicated is unspecified; the other four displayed images of St. Agatha, Our Lady of Washington, St. Margaret, and SS. Perpetua and Felicitas. Our Lady of Washington, the central picture in this apse, depicts the Virgin kneeling with a model of the National Shrine floating before her. The Madonna was modelled by de Henwood on a statue also called Our Lady of Washington which had been erected between the entrance doors to the chapel in Caldwell Hall in 1889, and is still in place there as Patroness of Catholic University.[9] In the east apse, the central altar held a copy of the *Madonna of the Harpies* by Andrea del Sarto; only two other saints were identified, St. Catherine of Alexandria and St. Anastasia. In the north apse, the central altar retained the Immaculate Conception of the original decorative scheme. It was flanked on the right by St. Elizabeth and St. John the Evangelist, and on the left by St. Joseph and St. Anne. With some minor modifications in subjects and in placement, this scheme is essentially that for the mosaics actually on the altars, which were designed by Bancel LaFarge from 1925 to 1931.

The most obvious alteration in the program was the elimination of images of the Virgin from the central altars in the three apses. In the west and east apses the ten altars were dedicated entirely to early Christian virgin saints and martyrs. In the north apse, the image of the Immaculate Conception was replaced by a representation of the Good Shepherd; St. Anne, St. John, St. Joseph, and St. Elizabeth were retained. All five altars of this central apse are intimately connected to the principal theme ex-

4

II. ST. LUCY

pressed in the vault, Fulfillment in Christ born of Mary. The saints allude to Christ's human family and earthly mission, while the Good Shepherd is to be understood both as Christ and as the eternal Logos. He is Christ, the "divine-Logos-Shepherd, who carries mankind upon His shoulders, has redeemed men through His death and leads them home through every danger to the Father.[10]"

The Good Shepherd is, in addition, the most common representation of Christ found in the catacombs and among early Christians. As such the image is eminently appropriate for the decorative theme of the Crypt Church which is intentionally Early Christian in its form and in the details of its iconographic theme. Images and texts were selected for the vaults and for the altars because of their assocations with early Christianity and with the Roman catacombs. Then those images and those texts were expressed in an Early Christian style. The martyrs on the ten altars of the west and east apses are an elaboration of the theme of Fulfillment in the Church through the Holy Spirit, manifest, as it were, through early Christian exemplars of that theme.

The mosaics in the Crypt Church were "conceived in the same spirit as those glorious old mosaics of San Vitale and S. Appolonare [*sic*] in Classe in Ravenna," remarked a writer in *Salve Regina*, an early official publication of the National Shrine at the time of the unveiling of the last two altarpieces by LaFarge in 1931.[11] And indeed, the representations of the saints, particularly because of the elaborate materials of their costumes, do bring to mind the attendants to the Empress Theodora in the mosaic in S. Vitale. But they also evoke the figures from the procession of female saints and the prophets in the upper register in Sant'Apollinare Nuovo. The altarpiece of the Good Shepherd in composition is similar to the *Christ Separating the Sheep from the Goats*, also in Sant'Apollinare Nuovo, where the figure of Christ in the center is flanked symmetrically by two angels and the animals. But the picture should also be seen contextually in relation to the lunette of *Christ as the Good Shepherd* in the mausoleum of Galla Placidia, which is the most famous rendering of that subject in mosaic. These works in Ravenna, it is worth noting, were all executed in the fifth and sixth centuries A.D.

Though LaFarge has modeled himself upon these prototypes for the altarpieces in the Crypt Church, the works themselves cannot be confounded with sixth-century mosaics. What separates them from their models, what gives them their individuality is a tendency toward realism in the handling of the figures, which is characteristic of all post-Renaissance mosaics, combined with a stylized simplification and preciousness typical of much late nineteenth-century and early twentieth-century decorative art. The lessons learned from late Pre-Raphaelite and Art Nouveau artists —Edward Burne-Jones and Louis C. Tiffany—make themselves felt in the elegant placement of the figure against the plain glittering gold ground. LaFarge created a manner in these altarpieces which would convey the reality of the figures represented, respect the flatness of the mosaic panel, and at the same time acknowledge the iconic and decorative traditions in which mosaics as an expressive medium had developed. In the altarpiece of the Good Shepherd these qualities are epitomized. The figure of Christ is three dimensional and realistic. He is flanked by two angels whose realistic representation is qualified by the stylized patterning and placement of their wings. The composition sits on the surface of the panel as a design made up of a number of symmetrically arranged, elegant, and colorful forms. The conflict between the reality of the Christ figure and the artifice of the work of art is not resolved and is not intended to be resolved. The reality of the Christ—and of the saints in the other altarpieces —hovers consequently in an ambiguous realm against the gold background, alternately acquiring and losing real presence in the flickering half-light of the crypt. LaFarge has captured something of the quality of Early Christian mosaics in his altarpieces and as such they are eminently suited to the catacomb-like atmosphere of the Crypt Church. However, it should be emphasized that Early Christian mosaics were only a starting

7

point. They provide a key, so to speak, within which the artist goes on to create modern and unique works.

The inspiration for using an Early Christian style for the Crypt Church came in large part from Bishop Shahan whose interest in that period of church history is well documented in his book, *The Blessed Virgin in the Catacombs*. And behind Bishop Shahan, one can see the influence of Cardinal Caesar Baronius who in his monumental history, the *Annales Ecclesiatici*, gave voice to the importance placed on early Christian traditions within the Counter-Reformation Church of the late sixteenth century. Baronius's approach was grounded in a search for historical authenticity as manifest in early Christian historians whose authority he accepted on the level of revealed truth. His respect for early Christian writers extended to all things early Christian. The discoveries of early Christian archaeology were considered revelatory of a true and original Christian state, and early Christian art was thought to be an aesthetic embodiment of a pure and direct religious expression. Within this context, the mosaic has a special significance, for it was the traditional medium used by early Christians for church decorations. It was largely through the influence of Baronius and his studies that the New Basilica of St. Peter in Rome from the late sixteenth century on was decorated in mosaics.

There never seems to have been any doubt that pictorial decorations of the Crypt Church were to be executed in mosaic. The altarpieces there set the pattern for using the medium for the principal pictorial decorations in both the lower and upper churches of the National Shrine, and the building was on its way in following the great tradition of mosaic church decorations which include S. Constanza in Rome, the churches and baptistries of Ravenna, the cathedral of Monreale, St. Mark's in Venice, and the Basilica of St. Peter in the Vatican.

There was a break in the construction of the National Shrine of the Immaculate Conception during the 1930s and the 1940s due to the Depression and to World War II which followed it. Work resumed in 1954 under the direction of the architect, Eugene F. Kennedy, Jr., and by 1959 the exterior of the Shrine had been completed. The dedication ceremony took place on 20 November of that year. Kennedy retained the Byzantine manner of the Maginnis plans for the church and together with it the idea of using mosaics for the interior ornamentation. In fact, work on the mosaics began as soon as it was feasible, and the Christ in Majesty in the north apse behind the main altar was in place for the dedication.

The iconographic scheme of the apses and the domes of the upper church dedicates the Shrine to the Virgin Mary under the auspices of Christ and the Holy Trinity. The original plan for the mosaics in the north apse would have made that immediately manifest. It called for a large image of Christ the Ruler—as Pantocrator—in the conch, with below a representation of the Madonna as Intercessor flanked by two angels. The scheme was to recall the powerful images executed in the cathedrals of Monreale and Cefalù in Sicily in the twelfth century.[12] In the architect's plans only the half domes of the apses were to have been covered by mosaics; the rest of the wall beneath the cornice was to have been veneered with marble slabs. One important result of the first decorations in the north apse was that they established that the entire surface above the chapels in all three apses would be given over to mosaics, a decision completely consistent with Byzantine interior decorative practices. The idea of the Pantocrator, however, did not prove to be satisfactory, because "it followed too closely a traditional and semi-petrified image so popular in the Eastern church." It was replaced by the actual image of Christ in Majesty, a representation of the enthroned Christ seen in the porticos of western cathedrals, such as the full-length figure of Christ, partially covered by a cloak and showing the wound in His side, on the Golden Portal of the Cathedral of Santiago de Campostela in Spain. The direct inspiration for the Christ in Majesty in the National Shrine, though, came from an eighth-century manuscript illumination which depicts Christ seated holding

9

both arms raised in order to display the stigmata in His palms.[13]

The dedication to the Virgin Mary, within the present iconographic scheme in the apse, is expressed principally by the Fifteen Mysteries of the Rosary which are represented on the altars. The north apse is devoted to the Glorious Mysteries; the west and east apses, respectively, to the Joyful Mysteries and the Sorrowful Mysteries. In this way the Virgin Mary's presence in this area of the Shrine, the sanctuary, is pervasive. She functions literally as well as symbolically as the Intercessor through whom the faithful approach the monumental Christ whose image dominates the whole church. The west apse, in addition, is specially devoted to the Virgin. In the conch she is shown as "the woman clothed with the sun," a concept taken from the Apocalypse of St. John the Apostle. The only other known mosaic representation of the theme appears in the dome of the Presentation Chapel in St. Peter's in the Vatican. In both instances a connection between the Virgin Mary and the Woman of the Apocalypse is implicit. They are understood as symbols of the Church.

The last of the three apses is dedicated to St. Joseph as Protector of the Church, Patron of the Ecumenical Council, and Model and Patron of Workers. In the first two of these triple roles the saint serves to elaborate the apocalyptic theme explicit in the other two apses, in the representations of Christ in Majesty and "the woman clothed with the sun." This important theme is given a resounding statement in the dome of the sanctuary where the Triumph of the Lamb is depicted encircled by the twenty-four elders in four groups of six, and by "the four living creatures," an eagle, an ox, a man, and a lion, symbolic of the four evangelists, SS. John, Luke, Matthew, and Mark. The text illustrated is also taken from the Apocalypse of St. John the Apostle (5:12): "Worthy is the Lamb who was slain to receive power and riches and wisdom and strength and honor and glory and blessing."

So far the decorations in only one other dome in the Shrine have been completed, the mosaic in the dome of the chancel representing the Des-

III. TRIUMPH OF THE LAMB

cent of the Holy Spirit commemorated in the feast of the Pentecost. The other three domes, when realized, will be dedicated, looking up the nave toward the crossing, to the mysteries of the Incarnation, the Revelation, and the Holy Trinity. Together with the scenes of the Creation and Last Judgment in the arms of the transept, the themes are distributed on the seven domes of the Shrine "like members of the Divine Body on the Cross." The narthex will be devoted to depicting the life and death of St. John the Baptist.

The chapels in the National Shrine with few exceptions—the Blessed Sacrament Chapel, the Founder's Chapel, the St. Pius X Chapel—expand the theme of Marian devotion and underscore the dedication of the Shrine to the Virgin Mary. The chapels are of various types. There are those, like the chapels of Our Lady of Siluva, Our Lady of Czestochowa, Our Lady of Guadalupe, and Our Lady of Bistrica, which contain ethnic or national reference and which honor the Virgin as she has appeared or has been revered in various countries around the world. This concept, it will be remembered, was first discussed in relation to the program for the altars in the Crypt Church where ultimately it was rejected in favor of an iconography more integral to the early Christian character and scheme of the entire decorative ensemble there.

Other chapels in the Shrine commemorate various historical and miraculous appearances of the Virgin Mary—the chapels of Our Lady of the Rosary, Our Lady of Mt. Carmel, and the Miraculous Medal chapel, for instance—or special titles with which she is associated—chapels of Our Mother of Perpetual Help, Mary Queen of all Hearts, Queen of Missions, and Queen of Peace. Often those chapels have been donated by religious orders to whom the Virgin for some special reason is most dear. Dominicans supported the chapels of Our Lady of the Rosary, St. Dominic, and St. Catherine of Siena; the Chapel of Mary Queen of all Hearts is a gift of the Missionaries of the Company of Mary (the Montfort Fathers); and the Vincentian Fathers, Sisters of Charity, and the Central Association of the Miraculous Medal are responsible for the chapels of the Miraculous Medal, St. Vincent de Paul, and St. Louise de Marillac.

The same general principles discussed in connection with LaFarge's mosaics in the Crypt Church are apparent in the mosaic decorations in the three apses and the domes in the upper church. However, the "key" now is no longer Early Christian. The decorative schemes and the stylistic details are instead determined by the Byzantine manner of the architecture. Obviously, it would have been inappropriate in this setting to have used anything other than a complimentary Byzantine-like manner for the mosaics.

The upper church is dominated by John de Rosen's figure of Christ in Majesty. Iconographically, the source for the image, as we have noted, is rooted in Romanesque sculpture and illuminations. Stylistically, however, the monumental figure derives its Byzantine "key" from the twelfth-century images of Christ as Pantocrator in the cathedrals of Monreale and Cefalù. Like them, the Christ in the National Shrine fills the space of the conch completely and, in a band below, is accompanied by a number of other figures—angels and the Virgin in the Sicilian examples. The frontal pose, the halo inset with flames in a cross pattern, the elaborate design of the folds of the drapery, the hieratic and iconic presentation of the figure are all Byzantine in inspiration. In addition, though, there is a post-Renaissance anatomical and three-dimensional realism in the rendering of the figure of Christ; the legacy of late Pre-Raphaelite religious pictures is evident in the strong patterning and the stylization employed in the depiction of the angels; and there is even a hint of William Blake's mysticism in the expression and physiognomy of Christ's head.

The power of this work brings to mind the mosaics designed by Edwin Blashfield for the main altar and the pendentives of the domes in the Washington Cathedral of St. Matthew. They are fine examples of American mosaic decorations of the period 1895–1925 and demonstrate ideally the blend of realism and stylization found in mosaics in the late nineteenth century. The history of the mosaics of that period originates in the Basilica of St. Mark in Venice. In the Cappella Mascoli there are fifteenth-century mosaics based on cartoons attributed to Jacopo Bellini, Andrea del Castagno, and Andrea Mantegna in which three-dimensional architectural space and realistic modeling of human figures stand in sharp contrast to the flat gold ground against which they are set. Modern art, as it were, has come into conflict with the traditional demands of the mosaic medium and a compromise has been struck which preserves the nature of the wall and the gold ground which adheres to it, and, at the same time, explores the realism of forms placed against it. The next step in the stylistic evolution of mosaics occurred in St. Peter's in the Vatican in the seventeenth and eighteenth centuries. The full pictorial possibilities of mosaics are exploited there in order to create an orchestration of the Baroque ideas on illusion and reality. It is no longer easy to determine what is real and what is illusion in mosaic domes in St. Peter's. The "walls" and the gold which previously defined them no longer exist. An infinite pictorial expanse opens up and the spectator is caught up in an illusion which might curiously be real. The viewer finds himself confronting, as he becomes adjusted to the scene and more sophisticated with regard to it, first of all a vision of the heavens which he understands as illusion, then as a painting, and finally as a mosaic.

By the late nineteenth century, there had been a retrenchment from this expansive Baroque style. The solidity of the gold wall was reinstated and against it there were placed forms and figures with a strong realistic presence. That realism, though, was modified by the gold ground which by its very nature set a decorative non-real tone, and by a controlling sense of stylization in design and pattern which further accentuated the artifice of the work. Blashfield's mosaics in St. Matthew's idealize that position brilliantly, and the mosaic of the Christ in Majesty—as well as the altarpieces in the Crypt Church—is within a direct line of descent.

It is from this vantage point that one should view the mosaics in the conches of the east and west apses, those depicting St. Joseph and the Woman of the Apocalypse, as well as the mosaic panels on the fifteen apse altars. Stylistically, the mosaics hover between realism and decorative stylization. It is a difficult balance to achieve and the emotional impact of the work depends upon a delicate thread of ambiguity which is not always conveyed.

The same Byzantine spirit underlies the decorations of the two completed domes. In classical schemes of the ninth to the eleventh century the only three themes used in the single domes of the churches were the Ascension, the Pantocrator, or the Descent of the Holy Spirit. But later on in St. Mark's, faced with the problem of having to decorate five domes rather than one, the artists used all three of the traditional themes and filled the remaining two with scenes from the legend of St. John the Evangelist.[14] Something of the independent spirit characteristic of the program of St. Mark's is evident in the freedom with which tradition and imagination have combined to fix the subjects and the styles for the domes in the National Shrine.

The Triumph of the Lamb as a theme had not been used extensively in dome decorations. One finds the subject, though, on the vault of the Holy Sacrament Chapel in the basilica of Torcello and on the vault over the main altar in S. Vitale in Ravenna. In both instances the Lamb is shown in a garlanded circlet supported by four angels set into fields of arabesque designs. The subject also appears in the apses of SS. Cosmos and Damian and S. Pudenziana in Rome. In the National Shrine, the dome of the Lamb follows the prototype suggested by the vaults in Torcello and in S. Vitale, but the angels have been moved down to the pendentives and have been replaced by the four groups of elders, counterpointed by the symbols of the evangelist. The composition has been adapted to the continuous expanse of the saucer shape of the dome, retaining a firm structure but acquiring thereby a greater openness and a more organic unity. The model for these modifications were typical Byzantine domes like those in Hosios Lukas and St. Mark's. Characteristically, these compositions have fixed medallion forms in the center around which the remaining elements are arranged radially. The subject, which in Early Christian and Byzantine churches is found more likely on a vault than a dome, has been adapted by Millard Sheets, the artist, to the traditional structure of dome decorations and then interpreted in a manner which relies for its impact on a strongly geometric and abstract design. The four groups of elders are the block-like arms of a Greek cross punctuated by the open, almost arabesque shapes of the symbols of the evangelists. The center medallion is the brilliant core around which the design coalesces, both formally and contextually. There is little realism in the highly stylized Lamb or the groups of the elders, and in contrast with most of the other decorations in this part of the church, this work functions through its ability to evoke almost by formal means alone the mystery of the Cross and the apocalyptic sacrifice of the Lamb.

The Descent of the Holy Spirit is a traditional subject for Byzantine domes, and one would have expected that the obvious prototypical composition with a medallion in the center and forms radiating from it would also have been adopted for the chancel dome. But perhaps it was rejected precisely for that reason, so as not to have two similarly composed domes in juxtaposition. There is a vestige of that structure in the gold circle at the apex of the dome and in the tongues of fire which seem to be descending from that point, but the principal movement of the composition is lateral around the rim of the dome where the figures through whom the viewer comprehends the narrative of the pentecostal event are placed. Max Ingrad's design, however, is not free from Byzantine associations. The domes in the narthex of St. Mark's, in which the center medallion is purely decorative and in which a continuous narration encircles the perimeter of the dome, immediately come to mind. As one has come to expect, again we find here in the mosaic of the Descent of the Holy Spirit a respect for the flatness of the wall combined with a certain realism and illusionism in the treatment of the figures, together with an acknowledgement of the iconic and decorative traditions of mosaics.

As one moves away from the sacramental core of the Shrine different iconographic and contextual concerns come to the fore. That, together with the more intimate quality in the nature of chapels, may account for the greater variety in style and approach which is apparent in the decorations of many of the chapels in the upper and lower churches of the Shrine. Aleksandra Kasuba's concerns in the Queen of Missions Chapel, for instance, are largely geometric and abstract. The formal design for the wall behind the altar enhances the parabolic nature of the wall and converts the movement implied by the parabola into an expressive element which draws all things to the center and to the figure of the Virgin Mary placed there. Kasuba uses strong basic colors in her composition, and gold is used only for the halo and the stars around the head of the Virgin and for the cross on the orb she carries. Millard Sheets, on the other hand, in the Chapel of the Blessed Sacrament, focuses on content and adopts a manner which conveys directly and easily the iconographic and narrative program of the decorations. The style is seen to advantage in the panel representing the Miracle at Cana where clear, somewhat generalized, simple shapes, and a rather narrow range of colors are used to create broad patterns which function effectively both as wall decorations and as expressive form.

The two panels by Vytautas Jonynas in the Chapel of Our Lady of Siluva are yet another example of the variety of styles one encounters in the chapels. His "post-cubistic" faceting of the surface of the panel creates boxes within which episodes and events can be depicted. The panels focus on a primary single figure, Christ in one and St. Casimir in the other, and the forms are well integrated into the general design which in muted tones of gray, green, blue and brown respects the two-dimensionality of the wall and the decorative function of mosaics. The panels, in fact, demonstrate how well contemporary styles can be accommodated to mosaic decorations.

In some chapels, the style of the decorations express the ethnic or national patronage or dedication of the chapel. That happens in several ways and in several degrees. In the Chapel of Our Lady of Czestochowa a hint of Poland is lightly suggested by the decorative bands around the base of the dome and the stained glass medallion. Otherwise the scheme for the decorations is quite conventional, using figures arranged hieratically around the perimeter of a gold-grounded dome. In the Chapel of Our Lady of Siluva, in contrast, the ornamental borders in the dome and the decorative motives in the pendentives were conspicuously adopted by Elskus Albinas, the artist, from typical native Lithuanian textile designs. Although here too the general scheme of the dome with the four set representations of the Virgin is rather conventional, the use of the decorative elements taken from Lithuanian folk art helps to create a distinctive mood. The Byzantine–Ruthenian Eastern Rites Chapel, one cannot help noticing, is particularly, and appropriately, "Greek" in spirit. The Madonna on the wall behind the altar is a modern version of the Byzantine *Virgin Orante* and the image is one of the most traditional that is to be found in the Shrine.

The mosaics in the Chapel of Our Lady of Guadalupe are especially interesting in this context. Mary A. Reardon has based her style on those of twentieth-century Mexican mural painters like Diego Rivera and José Orozco. Like them she employs a kind of primitivism which is consciously naïve and which permits exaggerated narrative and decorative effects. The figure of Juan Diego on his knees to the left of the Virgin is a good example of both these things. The pose and the expression of the figure portray an intense religious and emotional involvement; the cloak spotted with roses which are scattered from below the image of the Virgin shows how effectively a narrative element can be transformed as well into a decorative one. In a like manner, the rhythm on the south and north walls, in the processions of figures standing and kneeling, is punctuated and paced by the flames of the candles some of the figures hold and by the schematically rendered geographical elements in the background. The walls of the chapel near the entrance are a dark blue, but they fade and lighten as they get nearer to the altar and to the image of Our Lady of Guadalupe. She is the source of the light in the chapel and the aureole around her is the softest of pinks, peaches, and yellows. The overall impression is that of a small chapel in a Mexican church. That was an intentional aim of the decorations and it has been quite successfully realized.

In all situations, the method of making the mosaics in the Shrine has been rather standard. The artists submitted full-size cartoons of their designs to the mosaicists. The mosaicists in turn made tracings of the designs which were used then as models for the placing of the tesserae, the small pieces of colored enamel out of which the mosaic is composed. The tesserae were placed directly on the tracing, creating the picture face up, following the shapes and designs on the paper. The cartoon itself, which was kept close by, served as the guide and model for color. When the composition was complete, the artist was usually consulted. Changes and adjustments in design and in choices of colors could be made then. The mosaic was essentially an assemblage of loose tesserae at that point. The work was secured by covering it with glued paper which, when dry, became the temporary support for the mosaic. The piece was then divided into sections and keyed so that it could be reassembled on the site.

The wall on which the mosaic was placed was prepared with a coat of fine plaster into which, a section at a time, the keyed pieces of the mosaic were set, paper side up. Before the plaster was dry, the paper support was removed and the tesserae were worked directly into the plaster to obliterate the seams which might exist between the different sections. At the end some grouting was done, where necessary, and then finally the mosaic was cleaned of all plaster and paper which still adhered to the surface.

There were only two companies principally involved with the execution of the mosaics in the Shrine, the Ravenna Mosaic Company and Venetian Arts Mosaic which became Crovatto Mosaics in the early 1970s. On occasions, however, work was subcontracted to European firms. The Ravenna Mosaic Company had work done for them by the Peter Recker Mosaic Company in Germany, and Crovatto subcontracted some of its projects to studios in Rome and in Spilimbergo, Italy.

It should be obvious how important the mosaicists are to the final appearance and success of the work. The other factors which influenced the style of the mosaics were the degree of direction imposed on the project by the Iconographic Committee of the Shrine, the ideas of the architect for the general visualization of that program, and, of course, the architectural space and overall architectural design into which the mosaic was to be set. The architect, together with the Iconographic Committee, devised a detailed program for the decorations which was then submitted to the artist. In some cases a good deal of exchange went on among the artist, the architect, and the committee to work out the details of the scheme. For the decorations for the dome of the Descent of the Holy Spirit, for instance, Max Ingrand's original designs were discussed at length by the committee and the architect before the final sketches were accepted. Millard Sheets's designs for the Chapel of the Blessed Sacrament, on the other hand, underwent only minor modifications at the suggestion of the committee—that the haloes be eliminated from all but the figures of Christ and the Virgin Mary. In some instances, no restrictions other than those of the program itself were imposed—Kasuba in the Queen of Missions Chapel was free to visualize the program in whatever manner she wished. But in other situations, sketches of the decorations were made by Kennedy, the architect, suggesting quite clearly how the program should be realized. That was the case for the chapels of Our Lady of Siluva and the Miraculous Medal where plans and drawings of the scheme were submitted to the artists by the architect. The artists, of course, were responsible for working out the details of the project. An indication of the architect's involvement with the mosaic decorations in the Shrine can be gauged from the fact that he designed the mosaics in the niches of the chapels in the transepts, in the vaults of the aisles and the ambulatory, and on the baldachin, among others. As for the relationship between architecture and the design of the mosaics, there is no better example than the Chapel of Our Lady of Guadalupe. The undulating walls of the chapel were an architectural feature which Reardon acquired with the program. Within those limits, the artist was free to design her mosaics.

The process through which the mosaics were actualized in the final analysis, incorporated many elements: the traditions of the Church; the architects and the architecture; the artists and their styles; the history of mosaic decorations throughout the centuries; and the skill of the mosaicists. In the National Shrine of the Immaculate Conception these elements have coalesced into one of the most impressive displays of mosaic art to have been created in either Europe or the Americas in this century.

Notes

1. Kennedy, p. 28.
2. Archives of the National Shrine of the Immaculate Conception. Box A–7.
3. *SR*, 2 February 1922; and Kennedy, p. 271.
4. *SR*, March 1920; also Kennedy, pp. III ff.
5. *SR*, November 1920, May 1924, July 1931; Kennedy, pp. 84, 93.
6. For a detailed description of the Crypt Church see Thomas J. Grady, "The Crypt Church of the National Shrine of the Immaculate Conception," *The American Ecclesiastical Review*, 137 (1957), pp. 400–09.
7. Kennedy, p. 114; and *SR*, March 1920, March 1923.
8. *SR*, November 1924.
9. Kennedy, pp. 19–21.
10. Ludwig Hertling and Engelbert Kirschbaum, *The Roman Catacombs and their Martyrs*, trans. M. Joseph Costelloe (Milwaukee [1956]), pp. 181 ff; also Grady, p. 406.
11. *SR*, October 1931.
12. Archives. *Iconography Committee Report*, 1954, pp. 12, 16.
13. Archives. *Iconography Committee Report*, 1958, p. 18 and Appendix; Hildegard von Bringen, *Wisse die Wege. Scrivas*, ed. and trans. Maura Bückeler (Salzburg, 1954) Pl. 33, p. 81.
14. Otto Demus, *Byzantine Mosaic Decoration* (New Rochelle, N.Y., 1976), pp. 17, 68.

The Upper Church

Upper Church

1. Our Lady Queen of Ireland Oratory
2. Chapels of Our Lady of the Rosary, St. Dominic, and St. Catherine of Siena
3. Chapel of Our Lady of Siluva
4. Chapel of Mary, Queen of all Hearts
5. Chapel of Our Lady of Perpetual Help
6. Chapels of the Miraculous Medal, St. Vincent de Paul, and St. Louise de Marillac
7. Chapel of Our Lady of Guadalupe
8. Chapel of Our Lady of Czestochowa
9. Chapel of Mary, Help of Christians
10. Chapel of Our Lady of Mt. Carmel
11. West Transept—The Last Judgment
12. West Porch
13. East Transept—The Creation
14. East Porch
15. Chancel Dome—The Descent of the Holy Spirit
16. Sanctuary Dome—The Triumph of the Lamb
17. The Assumption of the Virgin, after Titian
18. The Immaculate Conception, after Murillo
19. East Apse
20. North Apse
21. West Apse
22. Chapel of the Blessed Sacrament and Our Lady's Oratory

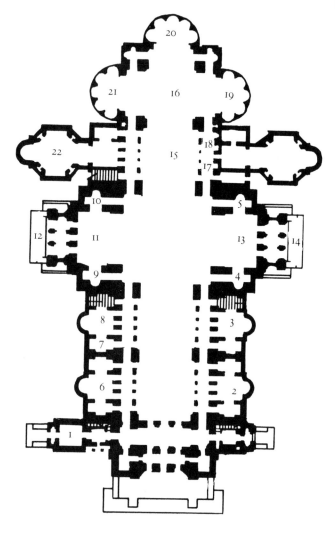

1. *Our Lady Queen of Ireland Oratory*

On the south wall of the Oratory the four symbols of the evangelists are set in mosaic into green marble panels. The images were reproduced from the illuminations in the Book of Kells, an eighth-century Irish Bible. The mosaics were designed by Harold Rambusch and Company, and executed by the Ravenna Mosaic Company. The Oratory was dedicated on 9 November 1980.

2. *Chapels of Our Lady of the Rosary, St. Dominic, and St. Catherine of Siena*

The dome decorations in this chapel contain, in a blue, blue-green, green field, a pattern of eight-pointed stars, symbols of both the Incarnation and of

St. Dominic through whom, according to Dominican tradition, the Virgin instituted the Holy Rosary. The four pendentives each contain the first half of the Hail Mary: HAIL MARY FULL OF GRACE THE LORD / IS WITH YOU BLESSED ARE / YOU AMONG WOMEN / AND BLESSED IS THE FRUIT / OF YOUR WOMB / JESUS. The mosaics were designed by Sister Thoma Swanson who also created those for the vaults and the altars in the chapels of St. Dominic and St. Catherine. In the vaults she employed again in the center a pattern of eight-pointed stars against a blue ground, flanked by two geometric patterns in shades of blue and green. The designs on the altars behind the bronze statues of the saints use a triangular motive, white on black with an overall gray diamond pattern, which was adopted from the Dominican shield. Over the statue of St. Dominic one reads the inscription TO PRAY / TO BLESS / TO PREACH; and over that of St. Catherine, ZEAL FOR / YOUR HOUSE / WILL DEVOUR ME. The mosaic ground behind the reredos in the Chapel of Our Lady of the Rosary, executed in tones of tan, brown, gold, and white, was designed by Eugene F. Kennedy, Jr., the architect of the Shrine.

Swanson finished the cartoons in 1968. In the same year the Ravenna Mosaic Company, which made all the mosaics in these three chapels, began to execute the work. The chapels, though, were not completed until February 1970. They were dedicated on 17 May of that year (*CS*; *MS*, May 1970).

3. Chapel of Our Lady of Siluva

The chapel, donated by the Lithuanian Catholics of America, commemorates the early seventeenth-century appearance of the Virgin Mary to the people of the town of Siluva, which led to the restoration there of the

Church after about fifty years of Calvinist suppression. The dome has a centerpiece of stained glass with a symbol of the sun, an emblem which often appears on Lithuanian wayside crosses. The glass is flanked on four sides by representations of the Virgin honored in Lithuania: Our Lady of Trakai, Our Lady of Vilna, Our Lady of Pazaislis, and Our Mother of Sorrows. Albinas Elskus, the artist who designed both the stained glass and the mosaics, incorporated elements of Lithuanian textile design in the ornamental border of the dome and of the pendentives, elements expressive of the native craft characteristic of much art in that country. Elskus also is responsible for the decorative mosaic field behind the altar which includes a border of pine cones and needles—Siluva means pine cones in Lithuanian; for the wayside crosses on the altar frontal, which again reflects a native craft popular in Lithuania; and the scene on the rear wall depicting the Statue of Liberty (symbolizing the United States) and a landscape with a tower (a monument to those who died in World War I—symbolizing Lithuania) with waves and a White Knight (Lithuania crossing the ocean) connecting them.

The two lateral mosaic panels were designed by Vytautas K. Jonynas. The panel on the south wall is devoted to St. Casimir, the Patron of Lithuania, who is shown in the center. Above are scenes relating two miracles attributed to him: the healing of a sick person through prayer, on the right, and on the left, the appearance of a mysterious horseman, as the result of St. Casimir's prayers, who led an army to victory. Also shown, on the left, is the baptism of King Mindaugas, the first Christian king of Lithuania, and, on the right, an architectural complex representing Vilna, the scene of much of St. Casimir's life. The panel on the opposite wall has as its theme Christ the Protector flanked by two angels, with the all-seeing eye of God above. References to persecution both past and present are intended by the representations of the parish church of Siluva, the Lithuanian landscape with wayside crosses, the scene of clandestine and domestic religious instruction, and by the episode in the lower right in which one sees Lithuanian exiles in Vorkuta, Siberia attending Mass. In the lower left corner one sees the Siberian

FIGURE 3

FIGURE 4

27

3. OUR LADY OF TRAKAI

4. ST. CASIMIR, PATRON OF LITHUANIA

prayerbook, composed and made by young Lithuanian girls in exile in Siberia.

Work on the mosaics in the chapel began in late 1964. Jonynas completed
the cartoons for his two panels by February 1965, and Elskus finished his
work by November of the same year. The mosaics were executed by Venetian Art Mosaic in 1965 and 1966. The chapel was completed in August and
dedicated on 4 September 1966 (*CS*; *MS*, August 1966).

4. *Chapel of Mary, Queen of all Hearts*

The blue mosaic in the niche, which acts as a background for the sculptured
reredos, was designed by the architect, Eugene F. Kennedy, Jr. The chapel is
a gift of the Montfort Fathers of the United States and of the Daughters of
Wisdom. Around the frame of the arch there are ten symbols of the Virgin to
which St. Louis De Montfort refers in his writings. Starting at the bottom
right, they are the Heart, the Lily, the Mystical Rose, "M" over an inverted
"V," the Crescent Moon, the Royal Crown, the Anchor and Rope, the
Morning Star, the Crossed Scepters, and an "M" and "R" joined. At the
apex is an image of the dove of the Holy Spirit. The symbols are repeated
down the other side of the arch in a different sequence. The stars, crowns,
and hearts, together with another symbol, the letter "M" over a cross, are
scattered also over the blue ground of the niche.

Work on the mosaics, which were executed by the Ravenna Mosaic
Company, was begun in 1963. The chapel was completed by August 1964 and
dedicated 1 May 1965 (*CS*; *MS*, May 1965).

5. Chapel of Our Lady of Perpetual Help

The sculptured altarpiece in the chapel holds a mosaic reproduction of the icon of Our Mother of Perpetual Help, a fourteenth-century painting which is preserved in Rome in the church of St. Alphonsus Liguori. The church is in the care of the Redemptorist Fathers who sponsored the decoration of this chapel. The mosaic reproduction was made in the Vatican Mosaic Studio. The mosaic in the niche behind the reredos was designed by Eugene F. Kennedy, Jr. Against a blue field, there are two decorative bands; from the one at the top a pattern of golden flame-like forms descend. Greek letters which are scattered against the ground identify the Child as Jesus Christ, the Madonna as the Mother of God, and each of the Archangels by name. The mosaic on the altar frontal, also designed by Kennedy, consists of a gold ground with "Chi Rho" in red in the center flanked by green vines and red and white grapes.

All the mosaics in the chapel, which was dedicated on 13 May 1962, were made by the Ravenna Mosaic Company (*CS*; *MS*, August 1962).

6. Chapels of the Miraculous Medal, St. Vincent de Paul, and St. Louise de Marillac

The cartoons for the mosaic dome of the Chapel of the Miraculous Medal were painted by Ernoe Koch upon designs suggested by the architect, Eugene F. Kennedy, Jr., who also provided the design for the mosaic in the niche behind the altarpiece. The decorations are comprised of a gold field into which twelve symbols of the Virgin Mary have been set. They are:

"Chi Rho" supermounting an "M"—Mother of Christ; crescent moon with a star and a crown—Queen Conceived without Sin; fleur-de-lis with an "M"—Mother Most Pure; winged heart enclosing an "M"—Help of the Sick; harp with a haloed dove at the top of a pillar, with a scroll bearing the litany title "Mater Boni Consili" in Latin—Mother of Good Counsel; conventional rose with an "M" in the center, a cross in the background, and three hearts intertwined at the base—Comforter of the Afflicted; palms surmounting a crown—Queen of Martyrs; crown with "Chi Rho" and medallions with Greek crosses—Queen of Apostles; lilies surmounting a crown—Queen of Virgins; crown with an olive wreath—Queen of Peace; lamp on a cushion against a large "M"—Seat of Wisdom; and an eight-pointed star over "Ave"—Morning Star. The pendentives depict four symbols of the Immaculate Conception: Noah's Ark, the Burning Bush, the Tower of David, and Jacob's Ladder.

The vaults of the two side chapels, dedicated to St. Vincent de Paul and St. Louise de Marillac, were designed by Nina Wheeler Blake. The first shows a Vincentian priest in front of whom there is a small stand with a number of FIGURE 5 scientific instruments, and a brother who holds a rake, references to Vincentian dedication to higher education and respect for manual labor. The two figures are surrounded by four men who represent aspects of Vincentian works. The priest is an allusion to Vincentian work in training the clergy; the poor man with a bowl, to work of charity; the native of Madagascar, to foreign missions; the nobleman, an indication that the Vincentians address themselves to all classes of society. The buildings in the background are the chateau of the De Gondi family in France where St. Vincent started as a chaplain, and the old cathedral of St. Louis, Missouri, once staffed by Vincentians and the scene on 20 November 1845 of the inauguration of the First Conference of the Society of St. Vincent de Paul in the United States.

The other vault depicts a Sister of Charity wearing the coronet, the characteristic headdress of the order. She holds a child to represent the work of the order among foundlings and unwed mothers. The group that accompa-

5. MISSION OF THE VINCENTIAN FATHERS

nies her illustrates other aspects of the order's mission: the doctor and the sick man represent work in hospitals; the young girl, work in teaching; the elderly woman, work in caring for the aged. The building in the background is the Novitiate of Emmitsburg, Maryland.

The mosaics in all three chapels were contracted by the Ravenna Mosaic Company, who had them executed in Germany. The chapels, which were sponsored by the Vincentian Fathers and Brothers, the Sisters of Charity, and the Central Association of the Miraculous Medal, were dedicated on 19 May 1963 (*CS*; *MS*, May 1963).

7. *Chapel of Our Lady of Guadalupe*

Our Lady of Guadalupe, Patroness of the Americas, is represented above the altar in this intimate chapel. On its undulating walls, two processions are shown approaching her. The walls are shaded from dark blue at the entrance of the chapel to pale blue at the sides of the image of the Virgin, who is contained within a pink, peach, and pale yellow aureole of light. The procession on the south wall contains representatives of the people of Central and South America, the one on the north wall representatives of the people of North America. The first figure on the south wall, kneeling in adoration and catching in his outstretched *tilma* the miraculous roses which were the sign of the divine presence, is Juan Diego, the Aztec Indian to whom the Virgin Mary appeared in 1531 and through whom she made her request for a church in Guadalupe dedicated to her. He is followed by Don Fray Juan de Zumarraga, Bishop of Mexico at that time; a Spanish conquistador; Sor Juana Inez De La Cruz, a seventeenth-century poetess; an Aztec chief; a South American family—father, mother, and daughter; St. Rose of Lima; an architect, representing professional people; a Mayan couple with a baby, from Gua-

FIGURE 6

6. OUR LADY OF GUADALUPE *(detail)*

7. PROCESSION OF PILGRIMS *(detail)*

temala; St. Mariana of Ecuador; a man from Peru; a woman from Bolivia; St. Martin de Porres; a workman; and two gauchos from Argentina. In the background are the mountains of Mexico, trees to indicate the jungles of Brazil, and the Andes.

FIGURE 7   On the north wall, the procession starts with two kneeling Mexican pilgrims. Then come a Mayan woman from Yucatan; a Spanish-American couple; a matador, representing all athletes; Mother Seton; a Negro and a Chinese citizen of the United States; St. Frances Cabrini; a miner; a North American family—father, mother, and son; the Venerable Kateri Tekakwitha; a Canadian woodsman; St. Isaac Jogues; and an Eskimo. In the background is the Basilica of Our Lady of Guadalupe, the Grand Canyon, and the Canadian Rocky Mountains.

There are two inscriptions. The one which runs along the bottom of the south wall reads, WHO IS SHE THAT COMES FORTH LIKE THE RISING DAWN FAIR AS THE MOON BRIGHT AS THE SUN; and the one at the bottom of the north wall, LIKE THE RAINBOW GLEAMING AMID LUMINOUS CLOUDS * LIKE THE BLOOM OF ROSES IN THE SPRING.

The cartoons for the decoration of this chapel, created by Mary A. Reardon, were begun in 1964. The work is signed under the gauchos on the south wall. The mosaics, which were made by the Ravenna Mosaic Company, were completed by September 1965, but the chapel was not dedicated until 22 April 1967 (CS; MS, February 1966, May 1967).

8. Chapel of Our Lady of Czestochowa

The chapel was sponsored by the Polish-American parishes in the United States and contains on the altar a replica of the picture of Our Lady of Czestochowa which, according to tradition, had been painted by St. Luke the

Evangelist. In the center of the dome is an image in stained glass of the Polish eagle. Around it there is a gold mosaic field containing representations of twenty people closely associated with "Poland's love for God and His Blessed Mother." They are: St. Casimir, one of the patrons of Poland, and a patron of young men; St. Stanislaus Szczepanow, the principal patron of Poland; St. Adalbert, the Apostle of Poland; St. Stanislaus Kostka, one of the patrons of Poland, Patron of Novices; St. Hedwig, a princess, widow, Cistercian nun, mother of St. Gertrude; Bl. Bronislawa, a Norbertine nun, cousin to St. Hyacinth and Bl. Ceslaus; St. Hyacinth, a Dominican who introduced the order into Poland; St. Anthony Zorawek, one of the first hermits of Poland; St. John Kanty, a professor at the University of Cracow, Father of the Poor; Bl. Ceslaus, a great preacher and missionary; Bl. Ladislaus of Gielniow, eminent for devotion to Our Lord's Passion; Bl. Stanislaus Oporowski, a great preacher at the Shrine of Our Lady of Czestochowa; Bl. Vincent Kadlubek, a bishop who resigned to become a Cistercian monk; Bl. Salomea, a princess and a Poor Clare; Bl. Simon of Lipnica, a Franciscan who became a professor at the Cracow Academy; Bl. Kunegunda, a queen and a Poor Clare; St. Clement Hofbauer, a Redemptorist, known as the Apostle of Warsaw; St. Joseph Kuncewicz, Bishop of the Ruthenian Rite and a martyr; St. Andrew Bobola, a Jesuit and a martyr; and Bl. John Dukla, a Franciscan and confessor. Each figure is depicted with an identifying attribute.

FIGURE 8

Originally John de Rosen had been asked to undertake the designs for the dome. After he declined, because of illness, the project was undertaken by Ernoe Koch. The mosaic design set into the marble at the top of the niche was designed by Eugene F. Kennedy, Jr., as was the reredos executed in gold, bronze, silver, and white tesserae. Work was begun in 1963. The chapel was completed in early 1964 and was dedicated on 3 May of that year. The mosaics were executed by Peter Recker of Weg, Germany (*CS*; *MS*, May 1964).

8. POLISH SAINTS *(detail)*

9. Chapel of Mary, Help of Christians

The niche in this chapel is covered with a blue mosaic field at the top of which there is a triangle, representing the Holy Trinity, enclosing a hand of God the Father. The emanating rays represent the Holy Spirit. Scattered over the ground there are the papal tiara, the keys of St. Peter, and stars, which are to be understood as symbols of Christian souls.

The mosaics were designed by Eugene F. Kennedy, Jr., and executed by Peter Recker in Germany. The chapel, donated by the Salesians of Don Bosco, was completed by mid-1965 and dedicated 1 May 1966 (*CS*; *MS*, May 1966).

10. Chapel of Our Lady of Mt. Carmel

The niche of the chapel is covered with a blue mosaic ground against which are set the statue of the Virgin and those of six Carmelite saints. There is a decorative band at the top out of which flames emanate, and a number of stars are scattered over the field. There is a halo behind the head of the Virgin, and the saints are identified by inscriptions. On the right, they are St. Mary Magdalene of Pazzi, St. John of the Cross, and St. Teresa of the Child Jesus; on the left, St. Andrew Corsini, St. Teresa of Avila, and St. Simon Stock.

The mosaics were designed by Eugene F. Kennedy, Jr., and executed by the Ravenna Mosaic Company. Work began in early 1963, and the chapel was completed by September 1964. It was dedicated on 2 May 1965. The chapel was sponsored by the Carmelite Order (*CS*; *MS*, November 1964).

9. LAST JUDGMENT *(detail)*

11. *West Transept Vault—The Last Judgment*

In the mosaic of the Last Judgment, Christ is seen in the center in clouds of FIGURE 9 glory. Below him the world is being destroyed by fire, the mountains rent asunder. In the corners four angels with trumpets announce the last day, and on the right and left are groups of people who rise toward salvation. The group on the right is made up of recognized saints, led by the Virgin Mary. It includes SS. Peter, Paul, John, Teresa of Avila, Elizabeth of Hungary, John Vianney, Martin de Porres, Pope Pius X, Isaac Jogues, Thomas More, and Maria Goretti. The group on the left, led by three angels and St. Stephen, is of unrecognized saints. There is an eighteenth-century American man, a modern worker, an Oriental American, a frontier woman and child, an Indian woman, a businessman, a small boy, a soldier, and a monk. At the bottom there are five figures who turn away from salvation and suggest those who are condemned.

The cartoons for the mosaics were painted by Mary A. Reardon. They were completed by October 1971 and then executed by the Ravenna Mosaic Company. Work in the vault was completed during May 1972. The mosaic is signed under the group of the condemned. Both the west and east transepts were blessed on 3 November 1973 (*CS*; *MS*, May, August, 1972).

12. *West Porch—Five Tympana*

Charity, the theme on the exterior of the west side of the Shrine, is expressed also in the five marble mosaic panels on the West Porch. The mosaics depict the Church's charity in America. The central panel shows Christ telling the story of the Good Samaritan. Those on the right depict the Sisters of Charity in a hospital during the Civil War (signed and dated FRANCIS BRADFORD 1958), and a chaplain on a battlefield consoling a soldier; those on the left, Father Damian and Brother Dutton on Molokai, and Sisters caring for the aged. The cartoons were designed by Francis Scott Bradford. The mosaics were installed in early 1959. In 1960 Bradford's designs were awarded the medal in mural painting by the National Academy of Design at the Exhibition of Mural Painting and Architecture in New York (*SR*, November 1959, February 1959).

13. *East Transept Vault—The Creation*

FIGURE 10   The Creation mosaic portrays the six days of God's creation according to Genesis. The hand of the Creator and the figures of Adam and Eve dominate the center of the composition. Below them, encased in the earth, there is an image of a human foetus, symbolizing the dust out of which man was raised, and at the top there is a broad area which represents the expanses of the universe. On the left are the waters and the living creatures associated with them. Included are prehistoric fish, a shark, and a manta ray. There is a polar bear who has emerged from the water, and flying overhead a number of birds. Below this group, in the two corners, there are DNA symbols, indications of a basic unit of living matter out of which all life could have evolved. On the right one sees the earth dominated by a volcano with a variety of plants and animals. There is a dinosaur and monkeys, a lion, a giraffe, a cow, and a lamb.

The commission for this work initially had been given to Ernoe Koch. After his death it was assumed by Mary A. Reardon who completed the cartoons by the end of August 1972. The mosaics, which were executed in Italy

10. CREATION *(detail)*

II. FATHER STEPHEN BADIN, APOSTLE OF KENTUCKY

and then installed by the Ravenna Mosaic Company, were completed by September 1973. The mosaic is signed MARY REARDON in the lower right. A blessing of both the east and west transepts took place on 3 November of the same year (*MS*, November 1973).

14. *East Porch—Five Tympana*

Faith, the theme of the decorations for the exterior of the east side of the Shrine, is carried through into the five marble mosaics on the East Porch. The central panel depicts Christ teaching, with an accompanying inscription which reads RENDER TO CAESAR THE THINGS THAT ARE CAESAR'S—UNTO GOD THE THINGS THAT ARE GOD'S. The other four panels commemorate the coming of the faith to America. From left to right, they show the founding of the city of St. Augustine and the first Catholic parish in America; the first ordained priest in the United States, Stephen Badin, FIGURE 11 called the Apostle of Kentucky; Father Eusebio Kino, the Padre on Horseback; and Father Junipero Serra founding the mission at Monterey. This last lunette is signed JOHN DE ROSEN, the artist who designed the cartoons. The mosaics were installed in early 1959 (*SR*, February 1959).

15. *Chancel Dome—The Descent of the Holy Spirit*

The chancel dome represents the Descent of the Holy Spirit on the feast of FIGURE 12 the Pentecost. Against a gold ground, the brilliant red tongues of fire descend upon groups of people situated around the rim of the dome. The principal group contains the Virgin Mary and six apostles. The other apostles are depicted in the trio on the right, a single figure, and the men on the left. On the back part of the dome three groups of ordinary people, men, women, and children, also receive the Holy Spirit as it descends. The theme continues into the four pendentives where the tongues of fire fall upon representations of the four parts of the world: Europe, depicted heir to the Mediterranean classical world; Asia, as a Buddhist monk; Africa; and America. The inscriptions that run around the base of the dome read: JESUS HAS POURED FORTH THIS SPIRIT YOU SEE AND HEAR (*Acts* 2:33); IN THESE DAYS I WILL POUR OUT MY SPIRIT UPON ALL MANKIND (*Joel* 1:2); SEND FORTH YOUR SPIRIT AND RENEW THE FACES OF THE EARTH (*Psalm* 103:30); THE SPIRIT OF THE LORD FILLS THE WORLD AND GOVERNS ALL (*Wisdom* 7:24–8:1).

FIGURE 13

The cartoons for the dome were painted by Max Ingrand, who had started working on them in 1966. The mosaics, executed by the Ravenna Mosaic Company, were completed in April 1968 (*CS*; *MS*, August 1968).

16. Sanctuary Dome—The Triumph of the Lamb

PLATE III

FIGURE 14

The dome is dominated by the symbol of the mystical Lamb of the Apocalypse surrounded by a circle of red and gold flames set into a blue field in which there is a scattering of golden stars. The Lamb's heart is bleeding, and he is represented with seven horns and seven eyes, symbolic of the seven spirits of the Lord sent out into the world. There is a scroll at his feet. The twenty-four elders who accompany the Lamb in the vision of St. John are represented in four groups of six, forming a Greek cross with the Lamb in the center. Placed between the groups of the elders are the symbols of the four evangelists: the lion of St. Mark, the eagle of St. John, the human figure of St. Matthew, and the ox of St. Luke. In each of the pendentives, there is an

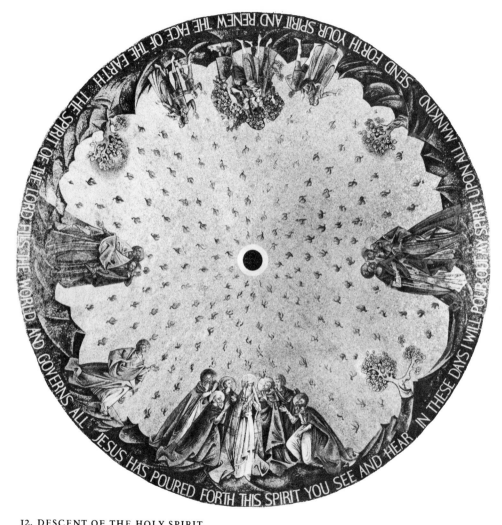

12. DESCENT OF THE HOLY SPIRIT

13. PERSONIFICATION OF ASIA

angel holding a globe showing the four corners of the earth with inscriptions which indicate Christ's reign over the whole world. The earth seen from the south is accompanied by the inscription WORD OF GOD; from the north, SON OF GOD; from the east, LORD OF LORDS; and from the west, KING OF KINGS. The inscriptions which run around the base of the dome read: WORTHY IS THE LAMB WHO WAS SLAIN TO RECEIVE POWER AND RICHES; WORTHY IS THE LAMB WHO WAS SLAIN TO RECEIVE WISDOM AND STRENGTH; WORTHY IS THE LAMB WHO WAS SLAIN TO RECEIVE HONOR AND GLORY; WORTHY IS THE LAMB WHO WAS SLAIN TO RECEIVE BLESSING. They all derive from the hymn of the elders, the living creatures, and the angels in The Apocalypse of St. John the Apostle (4:11 and 5:12–13).

The cartoons for the dome were painted by Millard Sheets in 1964 and 1965. The mosaics were executed by the Ravenna Mosaic Company and were completed in December 1966. The dome was a gift from Polish-American Catholics (*CS*; *MS*, May 1967).

17. *The Assumption of the Virgin*

The mosaic is based on the top part of the painting by Titian in the church of S. Maria Gloriosa dei Frari, Venice. The panel was made by the Vatican Mosaic Studio under the initial order of Pope Pius XII. After his death Pope John XXIII confirmed the gift. The mosaic arrived at the Shrine in March 1960 and was placed at that time on the west wall in the nave of the upper church. It was moved to its present location near the entrance to the sacristy in June 1962 (*EH*; *MS*, August 1960).

14. TRIUMPH OF THE LAMB *(detail)*

18. The Immaculate Conception

FIGURE 15

The gift of this mosaic copy of the painting by Bartolomè Estaban Murillo in the Prado in Madrid was announced by Pope Benedict XV in 1919 at about the same time that the plans for the National Shrine were being actualized. However, the project was suspended because of the Pope's death in 1922, and it was not until late 1923 that Pope Pius XI confirmed the gift and ordered the Vatican Mosaic Studio to begin work on it. In 1924 Carlo Muccioli, the director of the mosaic studio, went to Madrid to complete the copy after the Murillo which was to be used as the cartoon for the mosaic. The other mosaicists who worked on the panel were Luigi Chiaserotti, Ludovico Lucietto, and Romolo Sellini. Work on the mosaic, except for pointing and polishing, was finished by June 1929, but the piece did not arrive at the Shrine until 17 June 1930. The mosaic at first was kept in the Crypt Church. It was then moved to a spot in the upper church near the entrance to the future Chapel of the Blessed Sacrament. In June 1967 it was placed in the present location, paired with the mosaic of the Assumption of the Virgin (*SR*, March 1929, January 1930, May 1930).

19. East Apse

The east apse is dedicated to St. Joseph as Protector of the Church, as Patron of the Second Ecumenical Council, and as Model and Patron of Workers. The first theme is expressed in the figure of St. Joseph holding the Christ Child, which dominates the conch; in the other elements of that grouping —the landscaping symbolizing Joseph as the just man, "like a tree planted

15. IMMACULATE CONCEPTION *(after Murillo)*

near running waters, which brings forth its fruit in due season" (*Psalm* 1:3); and in the family group consisting of father, mother, son, and daughter, a reference to Joseph's position as foster father to Christ, to the Church, and, by extension, a model for fathers and for family life. In effect, St. Joseph as Patron of the Second Ecumenical Council, depicted on the right, is a manifestation of his more universal role as Protector of the Church: the Council takes place under his universal protection and under his specific patronage. The group portrays Pope John XXIII together with nineteen members and observers of the Council. Gathered around Pope John XXIII on the left are: Archbishop Josyf Slipyi of Lwow; Agostino Cardinal Bea, President of the Secretariat for Promoting Christian Unity; Sister Mary Luke, an observer from the United States; Giovanni Battista Cardinal Montini, Archbishop of Milan (later Pope Paul VI); Francis Cardinal Spellman of New York; Maximus IV Saigh, Melkite Patriarch; Archpriest Vitali Borovoi, Russian Orthodox observer; Leo Joseph Cardinal Suenens, Archbishop of Malines-Brussels; Bishop Petar Cule of Mostar, Yugoslavia; Alfredo Cardinal Ottaviani, President of the Holy Office. And on the right, reading down: Dr. Kristan E. Skydsgaard, Lutheran observer from Denmark; Laurian Cardinal Rugambwa of Bukoba, Tanganyika; Paul-Emile Cardinal Leger, Archbishop of Montreal; James Norris, Catholic lay observer from the United States; John Courtney Murray, S.J., Council expert; Valerian Cardinal Gracias of Bombay; Bishop Oetro Arikata Kobayashi of Sendai, Japan; Archbishop Miguel Dario Miranda y Gomez of Mexico City; and Bishop Tulio Botero Salazar of Medellin, Columbia.

Along the bottom of the mosaic various workers are represented, illustrative of the other principal theme of the decorations. From left to right one recognizes a man emptying trash, a young woman scrubbing steps, an older woman resting from her scrubbing, a carpenter, a welder and a repairman in conversation, two women picking apples, three fishermen drawing a net, three men laying a cable, a woman and two men in a field, a man shearing sheep, a woman carding wool, and a woman washing clothes.

On the soffit of the arch the Holy Family is shown on its flight to Egypt. On the north end there is a desert scene with palm trees, the Sea of Galilee, and a fisherman; on the south end, a scene with palm trees, pyramids, an ibis, and the Nile.

The chapels in the east apse are devoted to the five Sorrowful Mysteries of the Rosary. As in the other two apses, the panels are divided by an inscription above which there is a depiction of the Mystery, while below an Old Testament prototype for the Mystery is illustrated. From left to right, the altarpieces represent the Agony in the Garden with Christ and three sleeping apostles, with below a scene of the expulsion of Adam and Eve from the Garden of Eden (*Gen.* 2:23–24). The inscription reads SEE IF THERE IS ANY SUFFERING LIKE MINE (*Lam.* 1:12). The next shows the Flagellation of Christ. The inscription is BY HIS CHASTISEMENT WE WERE HEALED (*Is.* 53:5), and the lower panel shows Jeremiah being whipped because it was mistakenly assumed that he was a traitor (*Jer.* 37:13–20). The center altar portrays the Crowning with Thorns; the inscription reads THE BREATH OF OUR LIFE WAS HELD A PRISONER (*Lam.* 4:26), and the lower panel depicts King Joachim taken prisoner by the Babylonians (4 *Kings* 24:12–15). Then follows the Carrying of the Cross, paralleled to Isaac carrying the wood for his own sacrifice (*Gen.* 22:6–9), with the inscription THE LORD LAID UPON HIM THE GUILT OF US ALL (*Is.* 53:6). The last altar in the east apse represents the Crucifixion. The Old Testament prototype shows the Passover lamb being sacrificed (*Ex.* 12:1–6), and the text in the panel reads CHRIST OUR PASSOVER LAMB IS SACRIFICED (1 *Cor.* 5:7).

The artist for all the mosaics in the east apse was Austin Purves, Jr. He began work on the cartoons in 1964. They were executed by Venetian Art Mosaic, starting in late 1965, and were completed by December 1966. The dedication took place on 9 December 1967. The chapel is a gift of the Franciscan family (*CS*; *MS*, February 1966, February 1967, February 1968).

Christ in Majesty is represented in the conch of the north apse. He is shown   Plate 1
seated, enthroned, His arms spread, with the signs of the stigmata visible in
the palms of His hands and in His side. The clouds around His throne are
signs of His providence, and the water at the base of the mosaic is a symbol of
purification and salvation. Across the bottom of the mosaic, in copious red
cloaks, there are three Dominations, the fourth order of angels, wearing on
their breasts emblems of a tree, an eagle, and a cross, symbolizing respectively the ministry of temporal things, contemplation and worship, and the
ministry of spiritual things. They are flanked by two seraphim, angels of the
first order, and by four guardian angels dressed in white. The ones on the left
hold a model of the National Shrine and the sun; those on the right, the earth
and a scroll upon which is written the inscription ANGELE / DEI / ORA PRO /
JOANNE / PICTORE (Angel of God, pray for John the painter), a reference to
the artist John de Rosen who designed the mosaic here in the conch as well
as those on the five altars below. The apocalyptic nature of the image of the
Christ in Majesty is adopted from the Apocalypse of St. John the Apostle
(4:2–3).

    The five altarpieces in the north apse are dedicated to the Glorious Mys-
teries of the Rosary. The panels are divided by an inscription about which
the appropriate Mystery is represented. Below is a scene depicting the Old
Testament prototype for that Mystery. The first, going from left to right,
represents the Resurrection. The inscription reads HE IS NOT HERE FOR HE
IS RISEN AS HE SAID (*Matt.* 28:6), and the mosaic shows the angel announc-   FIGURE 16
ing to the three Marys that Christ has risen from the dead. Below is a scene
with Joseph being raised from the pit into which he had been cast by his
brothers (*Gen.* 37). The Ascension shows Christ in a medallion ascending in   FIGURE 17
the presence of the Virgin Mary and five of the apostles: I ASCEND TO MY

16. THREE MARYS AT THE TOMB

17. ASCENSION OF CHRIST

FATHER AND YOUR FATHER (*John* 20:17). The Old Testament prototype is Elias taken up to heaven in a fiery chariot (4 *Kings* 2). In the center is the Pentecost altar in which the Holy Spirit descends upon the Virgin and the twelve apostles. The inscription reads THEY WERE ALL FILLED WITH THE HOLY SPIRIT (*Acts* 2:4), and at the bottom is a scene of Moses on Mt. Sinai about to receive the Ten Commandments from God (*Ex.* 19:20 ff). The next altar is that of the Assumption which depicts the Virgin Mary in an aureole being assumed into heaven in the presence of three of the apostles, among whom the young John is recognizable. The inscription, WHO IS SHE COMING FORTH AS THE RISING DAWN (*Cant.* 6:9), separates the Assumption from a scene in which the Ark of the Covenant is being carried to the temple to be preserved (*Psalm* 131:8). And on the last altar on the right, one witnesses the Coronation of the Virgin by Her Son juxtaposed with the Old Testament prototype of Solomon leading his mother Bethsabee to a throne set for her to the right of his (3 *Kings* 2:19). The inscription here reads ON HER HEAD IS A CROWN OF TWELVE STARS (*Apoc.* 12:1).

The mosaic of Christ in Majesty, the gift of an anonymous donor, was executed in 1959 and was in place for the dedication of the Shrine on 20 November. It was made by the Ravenna Mosaic Company. The five altarpieces were designed by de Rosen in 1959 and executed in late 1959 and 1960 in Germany. They were completed by 12 November of that year when the dedication of the altars took place. The altarpieces were a gift from the Catholic Daughters of America (*CS*; *MS*, August 1959, November 1960, February 1964).

The theme of the mosaic in the conch of the west apse is taken from The Apocalypse of St. John the Apostle (12:1–6). The scene illustrates the episode where "a great sign appeared in heaven: a woman clothed with the sun, and the moon was under her feet, and upon her head a crown of twelve stars. And being with child, she cried out in her travail and was in the anguish of delivery. And another sign was seen in heaven, and behold, a great red dragon having seven heads and ten horns, and upon his heads seven diadems." The dragon is prepared to devour the child as soon as it is born, but he is saved by God and the dragon is cast down out of heaven. The woman is iden-   FIGURE 18
tified here with Mary Immaculate, but the connection must be understood as Mary in the broadest symbolic context; both Mary and the "woman clothed with the sun" represent the Church. The mosaic is signed J. YOUNG on the bottom left.

In the center of the soffit of the arch there is a vignette depicting the expulsion of Adam and Eve from the Garden of Eden. The scene is couched between two inscriptions which highlight Mary as the second Eve, and contrast the Church of the Old and the New Covenant: on the south end, THROUGH EVE DEATH; and on the north end, THROUGH MARY LIFE.

The chapels of the west apse are dedicated to the five Joyful Mysteries of the Rosary. The panels are again divided into two parts by an inscription. The upper scene depicts a Mystery of the Rosary and the bottom scene alludes to an Old Testament prototype. Starting on the left one sees the Annunciation, the inscription THE WORD WAS MADE FLESH AND DWELT AMONG US (*John* 1:14), and a scene of the Lord appearing to Moses in the Burning Bush (*Ex.* 3:2); the Visitation, the inscription HOW DOES THE MOTHER OF MY LORD COME TO ME (*Luke* 1:43), and a depiction of the Ark of the Covenant in the house of Obededom (2 *Kings* 6:10–11); the Birth of

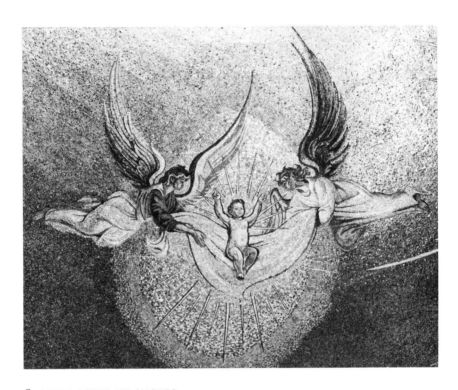

18. CHILD SAVED BY ANGELS

Christ with the Holy Family and the three magi and two shepherds, the inscription THE VIRGIN SHALL CONCEIVE AND BEAR A SON (*Matt.* 1:23), and Isaias before Achaz prophesying the birth of the Messiah (*Is.* 7:12–14); the Presentation of the Lord in the Temple, the inscription ACCORDING TO THE LAW THEY PRESENT HIM (*Luke* 2:22–24), and Anna presenting her son Samuel in the temple (1 *Kings* 1:24–28); and, finally, Finding the Boy Jesus in the Temple expounding before a group of teachers, the inscription ALL WERE AMAZED AT HIS UNDERSTANDING (*Luke* 2:47), with a scene showing Daniel as a young boy admonishing a group of elders for having unjustly condemned Susanna for adultery (*Dan.* 13:45–65).

The cartoons for all the mosaics in the west apse were painted by Joseph L. Young in about 1964. They were executed by the Ravenna Mosaic Company in 1965 through 1967 and were dedicated on 3 December of that year. The west apse was a gift from the Society of Jesus (*CS*; *MS*, February 1966, August 1967).

22. *Chapel of the Blessed Sacrament and Our Lady's Oratory*

The eucharistic theme of the chapel is stated in the figure of Christ crucified, which dominates the dome. Below Him stands the Virgin Mary receiving in an amphora the blood and water which flows out of His side. Twenty other figures, signifying people from all walks of life and all ages of Christianity, encircle the dome. The inscriptions which run around the base of the dome read: THE CUP IS SHARING WITH CHRIST'S BODY * THOUGH WE ARE MANY WE FORM A SINGLE BODY * A SINGLE BODY AS WE SHARE IN ONE BREAD. The representations in the pendentives symbolize the universal priesthood—the chapel was a gift of the bishops, diocesan priests, and seminarians of the United States. The scene with the Last Supper and the Multi-

19. MARRIAGE AT CANA

plication of the Loaves and Fishes refer to the Ordained Ministry and contain allusions to the eucharist. The other two are concerned with the Priesthood of the Laity. Represented in contemporary settings is the baptism of an adult on Holy Saturday and the confirmation of a young man and a young woman. In Our Lady's Oratory, there is a panel representing the Miracle at FIGURE 19 Cana, an event which has both eucharistic and Marian implications. The vaults are covered with a pattern of crosses set into circles and diamonds. In the center of the dome over the entrance of the chapel there is a large cross within a flaming circlet. The decorations in the chapel were begun in 1967 and completed in June 1970. The cartoons for the mosaics were designed by Millard Sheets and executed by the Ravenna Mosaic Company. The chapel was dedicated on 20 September 1970 (*CS*; *MS*, August 1970).

The Lower Church

Lower Church

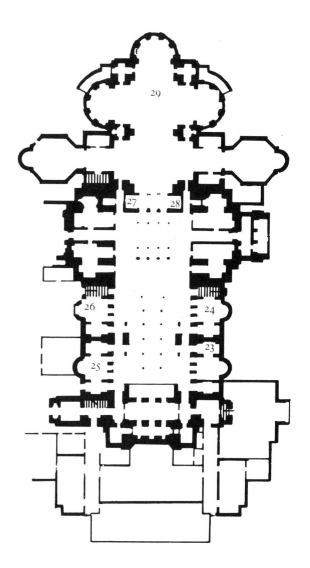

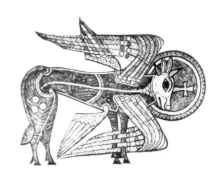

23. Chapel of Our Mother of Good Counsel

The small panel set over the altar is a mosaic replica by Ernoe Koch of a painting preserved in Genazzano, Italy, which, according to legend, miraculously appeared in the church there in the fifteenth century. Originally called the Madonna of Paradise, in the seventeenth century it also became known by its current title. The mosaic was executed by the Ravenna Mosaic Company. The chapel, a gift of the Augustinian Fathers, was dedicated on 26 April 1965, though the work on the mosaic panel dates from 1964 (*CS; MS*, May 1965).

24. Chapel of Mary, Queen of Missions

FIGURE 21   Mary as Queen and Protector of Missions is represented in the center of this mosaic designed by Aleksandra Kasuba. As in portrayals of the Immaculate

21. QUEEN OF MISSIONS *(detail)*

Conception, the Virgin Mary is shown with twelve stars around her head and with the crushed serpent under her feet. In her hand she holds the globe. The chapel was donated by the Oblates of Mary Immaculate, and in the groups to the sides of the Virgin are depicted the various people of the world among whom the Oblates in their missionary efforts have served. On the left one sees South Americans, North American Indians, Africans, and Orientals; on the right, Japanese, Eskimos, a Negro, and two children, the girl offering a rose to the Madonna. Kasuba painted the cartoons for the mosaic in 1965. They were executed by Venetian Arts Mosaic, completed in August and dedicated on 8 December 1967. The mosaic is signed A. KASUBA in the lower left (*CS*; *MS*, November 1967).

25. *Chapels of the Immaculate Heart of Mary and St. Anthony Mary Claret*

FIGURE 22   The mosaic panel on the south wall in the Chapel of the Immaculate Heart of Mary was designed by John de Rosen. It depicts Pope Pius XII in a red cape kneeling before the Virgin Mary who is shown clothed in white against a blue ground, and commemorates the Pope's consecration of the world to the Immaculate Heart of Mary on 31 October 1942. The inscription at the top of the panel reads WE CONSECRATE OURSELVES FOREVER TO YOUR / IMMACULATE HEART. The mosaic was executed by the Ravenna Mosaic Company. It was begun in 1965 and completed by September 1966. The chapel, a gift of the Missionary Sons of the Immaculate Heart of Mary (Claretian Fathers), was dedicated on 16 July 1967 (*CS*; *MS*, November 1966).

22. POPE PIUS XII BEFORE THE IMMACULATE HEART OF MARY

23. VIRGIN MARY AS "PROTECTION" *(detail)*

26. Byzantine–Ruthenian Eastern Rites Chapel

The chapel is dedicated to the Virgin Mary under the title of "Protection," FIGURE 23 which commemorates her appearance to the faithful in the Church of Vlacherna in Constantinople in 626 A.D. The Blessed Mother joined with the congregation in prayer for the deliverance of the city from destruction, and as a sign of her protection she spread her mantle over all those present. That mantle is symbolized in the mosaic, and from it emanates the light of the Virgin Mary's care and of her protection.

The mosaic on the south wall represents the cultural and religious background of Byzantine–Ruthenian Catholics in Eastern Europe. Against a background of the Carpathian Mountains with a wooden church characteristic of early buildings in that region, SS. Cyril and Methodius are shown bringing Christianity to the Slavs. Near the top of the panel is a copy of the weeping icon of Maria Povch from Hungary.

The mosaic on the north wall illustrates the presence of Byzantine–Ruthenian Catholics in the United States. It depicts the Statue of Liberty and the cities and countrysides in which the immigrants had settled. The gold-domed structure is the seminary of SS. Cyril and Methodius in Pittsburgh. At the bottom right are indications of the major means of livelihood of the new arrivals, and of their progress in education and in the professions. The three shields in the lower left contain the coat of arms of the first American bishop, Basil Takach, superimposed upon that of St. Nicholas of Myra on the right, and that of the Metropolitan See in Pennsylvania on the left. The icon of Our Lady of Perpetual Help is represented in the top part of the panel.

The mosaics and the rest of the pictorial decorations in the chapel were designed by Christine Dochwat. The mosaic behind the altar is signed in the lower right. The project was initiated in 1972, construction began in the summer of 1973, and the chapel was completed in September 1974. The mosaics were executed by Crovatto Mosaics. The chapel was a gift from the Byzantine–Ruthenian bishops and their congregations. The dedication on 6 October 1974 celebrated the fiftieth anniversary of the establishment of the Ruthenian Exarchate in the United States (*CS*; *MS*, May 1973, August 1974).

27. Chapel of Our Lady of Bistrica

The chapel is a gift, together with the Chapel of Our Lady of Peace, from the Croatian Catholics of the United States and Canada. It commemorates a statue of the Virgin which in the thirteenth century accompanied refugees who fled the Turks and settled in the village of Bistrica, near Zagreb. The mosaic, designed by John de Rosen, is composed of a green-blue ground and a decorative arch, in red, white, and gold, set with seven rondels. Clockwise, from the bottom left, the rondels represent: St. Nicholas Tavelic with Blessed Ozana Kotorka, examples of Croatian holiness; the baptism of a Croatian peasant, symbolic of the official acceptance of Christianity by Croatia in 640; Our Lady of Sinj, a reference to the shrine on the Dalmatian coast; the Croatian coat of arms; Our Lady of Trsat, a reference to the shrine on the Adriatic Sea reported to be located on the former site of the Holy House of Loreto; King Zvonimir wearing the crown sent to him by the Holy See in 1076; Aloysius Cardinal Stepinac (1898–1960), Archbishop of Zagreb.

The mosaics, executed by Venetian Arts Mosaic, together with the cartoons, date from 1968. The chapel was completed in August and dedicated on 17 October 1970 (*CS*; *MS*, November 1970).

28. Chapel of Our Lady of Peace

John de Rosen designed the mosaic background for the altar table and the statue of the Virgin. The ground is shaded from green to blue and contains at the bottom two olive trees, symbols of peace. At the top, two angels, clothed in white, support a crown over the head of the statue. The mosaics were executed by Venetian Arts Mosaic. Work on the cartoons and the mosaic was done in 1968. The chapel, together with that of Our Lady of Bistrica, a gift from the Croatian Catholics of the United States and Canada, was completed in August and dedicated on 18 October 1970 (*CS*; *MS*, November 1970).

29. Crypt Church—The Altars

On 16 January 1925 Bancel LaFarge signed a contract to provide the cartoons for the five mosaic altarpieces in the north apse of the Crypt Church. The mosaics depict the Good Shepherd flanked by St. Elizabeth and St. Joseph on the left, St. John the Evangelist and St. Anne on the right, figures relative to Christ's earthly family and mission. The Good Shepherd, the first to be finished, was completed by May 1926, and was set permanently in place in November of the same year. The other four panels were in place by Christmas. Each figure is presented against a gold background together with his or her name and attributes. There is also an appropriate inscription on each panel: St. Elizabeth (Blessed are you among women and blessed is the fruit of your womb. And why has this happened to me, that the mother of my Lord should come to me?), St. Joseph (The faithful man will be much praised

FIGURE 24

24. GOOD SHEPHERD

and he who is the guardian of his Lord will be praised.), St. John the Evangelist (And the Word was made flesh.), St. Anne (The tongues of the pious magnify your seed. And every joyful tongue preaches your child). On the panel of the Good Shepherd are the Greek letters $\overline{\text{IC}}$ / $\overline{\text{XC}}$ / NI / KA—Jesus Christ Conquers.

The altars in the west and east apses are dedicated to early Christian virgin saints and martyrs. From left to right, the altarpieces in the west apse depict St. Agnes (Behold I come to you whom I have loved, who I have sought after, whom I have always desired.), St. Agatha (Christian humility is far more distinguished than the wealth and pride of kings.), St. Cecilia (While the organ was playing, Cecilia sang to the Lord saying, Let my heart be spotless so that I may not be confounded.), SS. Perpetua and Felicitas (There will be another who will tolerate me, wherefore I indeed will tolerate myself for His sake.), and St. Anastasia (O Lord, you have filled your family with sacred gifts.). The St. Agnes and St. Cecilia were in progress by February 1927, and in place by September of the same year. Those two panels contain a diamond-shaped emblem which encloses the letters BLF, the artist's initials, and are dated 1927.

By December 1927 only the above seven mosaics had been completed, and from then on the records are silent for a few years. We can assume that the three remaining altarpieces for the west apse were completed before work was begun on the east apse. The altars in the east apse, again from left to right, are dedicated to St. Lucy (Grace has been spread by your lips, PLATE 11 wherefore God has blessed you forever.), St. Susanna (Blessed are the spotless on the way who walk in the law of the Lord.), St. Catherine of Alexandria (Receive the crown which the Lord has prepared for you forever.), St. Margaret of Antioch (Send forth your light and your truth; they have led me and conducted me on to your holy mountain and into your tabernacles.), and St. Brigid of Ireland (This is a wise virgin and one from among the number of the prudent.). We know that the last two mosaics, the St. Susanna and the St. Margaret, were set in place in June 1931, and on the basis of that information we can date the altarpieces as a group as having been designed and completed between January 1925 and June 1931. The altarpieces, which were gifts from various individuals and organizations, were all executed in mosaic by the Ravenna Mosaic Company (CC; Kennedy, pp. 100, 107; *SR*, May 1926, October 1926, February 1927, September 1927, July 1931).

Chronology of the Mosaics

1925–31	Crypt Church altarpieces
1929	*Immaculate Conception*, after Murillo
1959	North Apse, *Christ in Majesty*
	East Porch, tympana
	West Porch, tympana
1960	*Assumption of the Virgin*, after Titian
	North Apse, altarpieces
1962	Chapel of Our Lady of Perpetual Help
1963	Chapels of the Miraculous Medal, St. Vincent de Paul, and St. Louise de Marillac
1964	Chapel of Mary, Queen of all Hearts
	Chapel of Our Lady of Czestochowa
	Chapel of Our Lady of Mt. Carmel
	Chapel of Our Mother of Good Counsel
1965	Chapel of Our Lady of Guadalupe
	Chapel of Mary, Help of Christians

1966	Chapel of Our Lady of Siluva
	East Apse, *St. Joseph as Protector of the Church, as Patron of the Second Ecumenical Council, and as Model and Patron of Workers,* and altarpieces
	Sanctuary Dome, *The Triumph of the Lamb*
	Chapels of the Immaculate Heart of Mary and St. Anthony Mary Claret, *Pope Pius XII before Mary of the Immaculate Heart*
1967	West Apse, *A Woman Clothed with the Sun*, and altarpieces
	Chapel of Mary, Queen of Missions
1968	Chancel Dome, *The Descent of the Holy Spirit*
1970	Chapels of Our Lady of the Rosary, St. Dominic, and St. Catherine of Siena
	Chapel of the Blessed Sacrament and Our Lady's Oratory
	Chapel of Our Lady of Bistrica
	Chapel of Our Lady of Peace
1972	West Transept, *The Last Judgment*
1973	East Transept, *The Creation*
1974	Byzantine–Ruthenian Eastern Rites Chapel
1980	Our Lady Queen of Ireland Oratory

Typeset by The Cottage Press, Greenbelt, Maryland
Design assistance from William S. Peterson
Printed by Universal Lithographers, Lutherville-Timonium, Maryland